UNCLE SAM

Wants you!

Military Men and Women of World War II

Sylvia Whitman

Lerner Publications Company • Minneapolis

To Rat, a.k.a. Harriette Grant, great nanny and friend

The following people deserve special thanks for their help: Martha Abramson, Bob Baldridge, George Coar, Lou Curtis, BettyLou and Bill Folley, Charles Ives, Lee Lund, Sara McCullough, Suzie Noon, and Lee Saunders, who shared their memories in frank detail, despite the tape recorder on the table; Sandy Whitman, my father, who served in the U.S. Navy during World War II, although his humorous stories were too self-deprecating to make the book; Mary Cook, a Spar, and Florida Seagals Unit 91, part of WAVES National, who gave me leads and a warm welcome; the administrators of the Beardall Senior Center and Baptist Terrace in Orlando, who let me solicit interviews; Shanna Flowers, who kept me in cake and gossip; Mohamed Ben Jemaa, who carried a lot of books back to the Orlando County Public Library; and editor Margaret Goldstein.

LIBRARY OF CONGRESS CATALOGING-IN-PUBLICATION DATA

Whitman, Sylvia, 1961-
    Uncle Sam wants you : military men and women of World War II / by Sylvia Whitman.
        p.   cm.
    Includes bibliographical references and index.
    Summary: Describes the experiences of men and women in the United States armed services during World War II, discussing such topics as the draft, boot camp, stateside duty, and combat in Europe and the Pacific.
    ISBN 0-8225-1728-0
    1. World War, 1939-1945—United States—Juvenile literature.
2. United States—Armed Forces—History—World War, 1939-1945—Juvenile literature. [1. United States—Armed Forces—History—World War, 1939-1945. 2. World War, 1939-1945. 3. Soldiers.] I. Title.
D769.W45   1993
940.54′8373—dc20   92-14832
                                                                CIP
                                                                AC

Manufactured in the United States of America

1 2 3 4 5 6 98 97 96 95 94 93

Contents

TURNING CITIZENS
INTO SOLDIERS

The first 500 years are the hardest.
    —Army humor, 1940s

Wearing a blindfold, Secretary of War Henry Stimson stood beside a glass bowl and fished out a capsule. It contained a slip of paper marked "158," an unlucky number for 6,175 young men who were being chosen at random for military service. With that brief ceremony, held on October 29, 1940, in Washington, D.C., the first peacetime draft in American history had begun.

Just two weeks earlier, 16 million men aged 21 through 35 had registered for the draft. Each man gave his name and address and received a number between 1 and 9,000. If his number was called by the government, he had to serve in the military for one year. Anyone who evaded the requirement faced up to five years in prison and a $10,000 fine.

In 1940 some Americans questioned the need for a draft. Bloody World War I (1914-1918) was supposed to have been "the war to end all wars." Since then, the United States had limited its army to only 375,000 volunteers. In September 1939, World War II began when German dictator Adolf Hitler ordered his forces to invade Poland. In less than a

*As President Franklin D. Roosevelt (*left*) looks on, blindfolded Henry Stimson chooses a draft number.*

year, Germany had conquered Denmark, Norway, Luxembourg, Holland, and Belgium. Japan was also extending its empire by force, attacking China and other Asian nations. Still, many Americans believed the United States could help its friends in Europe and Asia—by supplying food, equipment, and weapons—without sending its own sons and daughters to war.

Other people urged the U.S. government to prepare for war. In the summer of 1940, two congressmen introduced a bill, the Selective Training and Service Act, establishing a military draft. Although a thousand demonstrators gathered outside the Capitol and sang "Ain't Gonna Study War No More," Congress voted the bill into law. News that Germany had marched into France and had launched an air attack on Great Britain influenced the vote.

Even though its allies were taking a beating, the United States remained on the sidelines at the start of World War II. The military enlarged slowly. The U.S. Navy, the Marine Corps, the Coast Guard, and the Army Air Corps attracted enough volunteers to fill their ranks—since many young men thought these branches of the service were elite and glamorous. At first, the draft supplied personnel only to the army ground forces—the infantry, artillery, and armor division.

Every month, Selective Service sent letters to thousands of draft registrants. The "greetings" (so nicknamed because of their first word) listed a time and place to report for screening. First, each man met with his local draft board, an unpaid group of businessmen, veterans, and civic leaders. Using Selective Service guidelines, personal information, and a physical exam, the board decided whether an individual would be more useful in the community or in the military.

Factory workers, for instance, routinely received deferments—permission to skip military service—since they were building tanks, ships, planes, and guns vital to the war effort. Draft boards also excused husbands and fathers who supported their families. Some jokers soon referred to babies as "draft insurance." Board members questioned a candidate closely if they thought he had married quickly just to avoid service. Sometimes people sent draft boards anonymous notes naming eligible men who were trying to shirk their duty. One Arkansas draftee who couldn't read asked his wife to write a letter about how much she and their seven kids needed him. Instead, she wrote to the draft board: "Just take him. He ain't no good to me. He ain't done nothing but raise hell and drink lemon essence since I married him eight years ago."

Draft boards ranked draftees from 1-A (qualified and in good health) to 4-F (unfit). Candidates rated 1-A traveled to an induction center for a tougher physical exam. At first, the army set very high standards, failing anyone with flat feet, weak eyesight, or less than half his teeth. Many 4-Fers were in bad health because of the poor nutrition and poor medical care they had received during the economic hard times of the 1930s. At 6-feet, 2-inches and 140 pounds, actor Jimmy Stewart was declared too skinny for the military. But his patriotism won him many fans when he went on a diet to *gain* weight. To remove any shame from a 4-F classification, the army jokingly announced it had rejected comic-book hero Superman. Because of his X-ray vision, the army explained, Superman looked through a wall, read the wrong eye chart, and flunked his physical.

AN URGENT CALL TO ARMS

On December 7, 1941, the Japanese Imperial Army bombed the American naval and air fleet at Pearl Harbor in Hawaii. Americans were shocked. The surprise attack killed more than 2,300 servicemen and destroyed or disabled 19 ships and 188 airplanes. Within a day, the United States declared war on Japan. In turn, Germany and Italy—partners with Japan in an alliance called the Axis—declared war on the United States. Suddenly, the War Department was scrambling to train, equip, and transport American troops to unfamiliar battle zones across both the Atlantic and Pacific oceans.

Volunteers jammed recruiting centers in December 1941, eager to defend their country. Different branches of the military competed for

Boston draftees say goodbye to civilian life in November 1940.

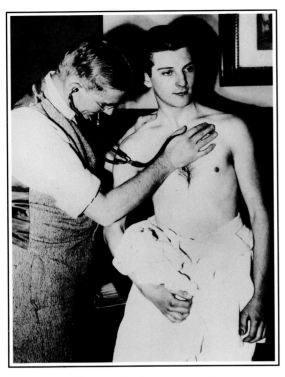

The medical exam—the first test soldiers had to pass

The government urged women as well as men to join the military.

talented enlistees. The navy lured young men with the slogan "Choose while you can." The military needed every volunteer—and then it relied on the draft to fill in gaps. Nearly 16 million Americans wore a uniform during World War II, the majority of them draftees. After Pearl Harbor, soldiers served not for a year but "for the duration."

The demand for able bodies prompted new definitions of the term "fit for duty." Soon men as young as 18 and as old as 45 had to register for the draft. Local draft boards periodically reclassified their pool of citizens, eliminating deferments for factory workers, fathers, and even prisoners. Instead of dismissing adults who couldn't read or immigrants who couldn't speak English, the army taught crash courses with textbooks such as *Private Pete Eats His Dinner*. Instead of disqualifying men with rotten teeth, the army fitted them with dentures. The number of army dentists increased from 250 in 1939 to 25,000 in 1945.

Although Selective Service did not draft women, about 350,000 women enlisted in the military during World War II. Female nurses and office workers had performed well during World War I, and the military needed extra hands once again.

About 74,000 women joined the existing army and navy nurse corps. The government also created new divisions for female volunteers: the WAC (Women's Army Corps), the WASP (Women Airforce Service Pilots), the navy WAVES (Women Accepted for Volunteer Emergency Service), the Coast Guard SPARS (named for the motto, *Semper Paratus*— "Always Ready"), and the Women Marines. Women were not allowed to fight in combat, but they filled almost every other military position from parachute rigger to transport pilot to air traffic controller.

Martha Abramson enlisted in the WAVES at age 20 because she wanted to travel, to learn nursing, and to contribute to the war effort. She ended up an office worker but still felt useful. "The main reason for joining during the war was to replace a male so he could go overseas and fight," she says.

Like many servicewomen, she had to overcome objections from friends and family, as well as bias within the ranks. Some Americans felt that women belonged at home—not in an "unfeminine" job on a military base. Male troops spread rumors, most of them unfounded, about the loose morals of female soldiers. Abramson explains:

> I think the only thing that made the men unhappy was they didn't care to see women in the service. Like I had a boy[friend] at the time, and he thought I was crazy. . . . He thought, "No, you're going to go bad. . . ."
>
> There was a bad reputation around the army gals and a little of the navy, [because a few] gals got pregnant and were discharged dishonorably. . . . Then there was the majority of women that held that uniform and really was proud of it. I know to stand and be in that uniform and salute the flag could bring tears to your eyes. To me, it was just such a great honor.

Men as old as 45, like some of these Chicago draftees, were called up for military service during World War II.

Male volunteers often shared that enthusiasm. Bob Baldridge from Omaha, Nebraska, could hardly wait to turn 18 in 1943 to follow his father, a World War I veteran, into the artillery. "I wanted to be part of a combat unit," he says. "I guess I was probably more gung ho than the average draftee."

Whether a chemist from Maine or a cowboy from Colorado, the typical draftee served not out of choice but out of a sense of duty. Many draft-age men didn't enlist. George Coar, for instance, had no desire to risk his life at age 18. "I had heard about how the planes came in . . . and the numbers of people that were killed near Pearl Harbor, and I wanted no part of that," he says. Nonetheless, when Selective Service drafted

Coar, he quit high school in the middle of his senior year to fulfill his obligation.

War interrupted many lives. Called up at age 30, Charles Ives left his wife and a job in an electric plant in Schenectady, New York. Entering the army stirred "more or less a feeling of anxiety," he says. "You just never knew what you were going to do the next day, or when you were going, or where you were going."

Although not always popular, the draft helped create a successful fighting force. As Bob Baldridge explains:

> That's one good thing about a conscript army, meaning a draft. . . . It's not a one-type of an army. Everybody isn't out of military school. . . . It's good to have representatives from all parts of the country, from all walks of life. . . . In time of real national emergency, you certainly would want a draft . . . not only to build up the number, the quantity necessary, but to give the army a nationwide feeling.

"THIS IS THE ARMY, MR. JONES"

Basic training, or boot camp, differed from service to service—and from unit to unit. But the goal of boot camp was the same for all the military branches. In a month or two, the armed forces had to teach civilians to think and react like soldiers.

The rite of passage began at reception centers, where the military processed draftees and enlistees alike. One of the first humbling rituals of army life was lining up for vaccinations—which inspired "Ode to the Medics" in *Yank*, a weekly newspaper by and for soldiers:

> They give me shots for tetanus;
> For typhoid, I get three.
> The yellow fever is an excuse
> For one more hole in me. . . .
>
> Oh, I haven't been in battle yet;
> In war I haven't starred.
> But if you saw the holes in me.
> You'd swear I'm battle scarred.

Next, members of the Quartermaster Corps (in charge of supplies and equipment) passed out army uniforms: three tan cotton suits, two darker wool ones, two sets of olive work fatigues, five sets of summer underwear, two winter sets, four pairs of socks, and two pairs of shoes—all "GI," or Government Issue. Soon the GI label applied to the servicepeople themselves. Around their necks, GIs wore twin metal "dog tags"—stamped with their name, identification number, blood type, and religion.

In the navy, sailors received uniform jumpers (shirts), slacks, and hats—white for summer, dark blue for winter. Women's uniforms in all the services resembled men's. Wacs, for instance, were outfitted in khaki shirts and skirts over GI slips and girdles. Regulations prohibited heavy makeup and jewelry other than a ring and a watch.

Most recruits complained about how poorly the clothes fit, but sergeants paid little attention. If a uniform buttoned, it wasn't too tight, they said. If it stayed up, it wasn't too loose. But quartermasters took great care when sizing a soldier's shoes, the most important equipment for the long marches ahead. Supply sergeants measured a draftee's feet at their widest as he carried two buckets of sand—a rough equivalent of an infantryman's 50-pound backpack. And, of course, GI fashion was not complete without the regulation half-inch haircut. Women wore buns or bobbed their hair above the collar.

Enlisted personnel scattered across the country for basic training. As Staff Sergeant A. L. Crouch wrote in *Yank*:

> If you live in the East, they will send you West;
> If you live in the North, they will send you South.
> What the hell does it matter? The Army knows best,
> So grab your luggage and shut your mouth.

Short on housing, the military stripped fancy rugs and chandeliers from large hotels and turned them into dormitories. It took over parts of college campuses, since the draft had cut into student enrollment. The army was also building and expanding training camps in the southeastern United States. There land tended to be cheap, the varied terrain suited training maneuvers, and nearby cities offered recreation. Often troops arrived before construction of the camp had finished, so they moved into tents amidst mud and dust. Boasting of their hardships, GIs at Camp Barkeley, Texas, described mosquitoes so big and choosy that they sat on a soldier's chest and checked his dog tags for his blood type.

Camps, which often housed more than 50,000 trainees, operated their own fire and police departments, sewage systems, and transportation networks. Rectangular wooden barracks rose no more than two stories high to limit damage in case of a fire. About 30 GIs slept on each floor, in cots lined up head to foot to prevent the spread of colds. Soldiers shared toilets and showers at the end of a hall. Many servicemen found the accommodations luxurious. In 1940, about one in three American homes had no running water. Some young men put on their first pair of shoes in the military.

Like many institutions in 1940s America, the army treated African Americans as second-class citizens. "I hadn't ever been in an environment where there was anything but segregation," says George Coar, who grew up in Orlando, Florida. "I was curious to some degree" if military life would be different. Most of the time, it wasn't. Blacks soldiers served in segregated units. They could not eat in the dining car on troop trains

The barracks at Camp Phillips, Kansas

but instead picked up boxed lunches by the back door. At camp, black servicemen slept in separate barracks. Shipped to frigid Cheyenne, Wyoming, for basic training, Coar shared the disappointment of many other black Americans:

> The thing that hurt me I think most, when I got there they had some German prisoners of war that they had brought back already, and overall they were treated better than we were.... They had excellent food.... Ours left much to be desired. They were treated with respect.

Waves on review at the Naval Air Station, Corpus Christi, Texas

Although black and white troops did not mingle, Americans of many different backgrounds roomed and drilled together at boot camp. Baptists from Georgia studied first aid, sanitation, and military courtesy beside Jews from New York. College students as well as eighth-grade dropouts learned how to read a map, pitch a tent, and defend against chemical weapons.

Women trained separately but similarly. Although officers did not instruct women on weaponry or combat tactics, female soldiers hiked in the rain and bathed out of their helmets just as male GIs did.

Marion Hargrove's popular *See Here, Private Hargrove* (1942) described the army's "Hardening Process," but no book could fully prepare civilians for the stress of boot camp. Muscles ached, officers shouted, and the person in the next bed often snored. The hardest lessons were often emotional. Trainees struggled with homesickness, discipline, lack of privacy, and prejudice. Southerners, Northerners, Christians, Jews, Hispanics, Italians, Poles, scholars, jocks, loners, and bullies teased each other and sometimes fought.

Prejudice usually gave way to tolerance, respect, and friendship, though. The bonds created at boot camp lasted through the war and sometimes into peacetime. When they first entered the barracks, recruits hardly understood each other's accents. When they graduated as comrades in arms, they spoke the same slang. Sailors called their mops "swabs" and their bathrooms "heads." Soldiers joked about the latest army "snafu"— Situation Normal, All Fouled Up. Although they left with some of the excitement and dread with which they had come, they were no longer alone. They belonged to a team.

"There's sort of a special kinship," Robert Rasmus explained in Studs Terkel's *"The Good War": An Oral History of World War Two.* "The reason you storm the beaches is not patriotism or bravery. It's that sense of not wanting to fail your buddies."

UNCLE SAM FOR A BOSS

A WASP trainee am I,
All sunburned and dusty and dry.
There's no time to play,
They work us all day,
Volunteers, but we'll never know
*   why!*

           —Women Airforce
           Service Pilots song

American soldiers needed specialized skills, so training continued in stages long after boot camp. Troops drilled for months, sometimes even years, in the United States. Wacs in a motor transport class practiced freeing trucks stuck in the mud, and paratroopers practiced jumping from airplanes. Infantrymen sharpened their rifle shooting, then learned to coordinate assaults with the heavy mounted guns of the artillery. After basic training in Wyoming, George Coar transferred to Fort Hood, Texas, to study tank destroyer tactics. Even at home, war was dangerous. Sometimes shells misfired or parachutes failed to open.

The military tried to match recruits' talents to their jobs. During induction, officers interviewed draftees about their work experience.

The army motor pool needed mechanics and truck drivers. Photographers joined reconnaissance units that gathered information about enemy positions. Hundreds of Navajo Indians trained as radio operators because they could send messages in their tribal language, which only a handful of non-Navajos understood. Mechanics entering the navy ended up as machinist mates, secretaries became clerks called yeomen, and doctors and nurses served in the hospital corps. Any man whose peacetime job had no use in war usually ended up in the front lines as a combat soldier.

Aptitude tests also influenced a military career. As an Army Air Corps enlistee, Lee Saunders could have headed in one of three directions: aerial photography, plane mechanics, or communications. Because of his musical background, he excelled on the communications test. After boot camp, he traveled to South Dakota for classes in radio mechanics and Morse code.

The interview process helped determine where a soldier was most needed in the military.

Recruits who did well on the Army General Classification Test could apply to Officer Candidate School. Before the war, military academies had supplied the army and navy with most of their officers. In the 1940s, as the armed forces grew rapidly, commanders found other ways to tap young people with leadership potential. College students often received officer training. The navy's V-7 program, for instance, turned recent college graduates into officers in just four months.

Wacs served in the United States and overseas in hundreds of different job categories, but most military women were shunted to traditional female occupations, such as office clerk or phone operator. Female doctors, rejected by the medical corps, pushed for a law that in 1943 finally permitted them to join the armed forces. Easily accepted by the service, nurses nonetheless had to fight for rank and salary equal to that of men with similar skills and education. Although the 1,078 Women Airforce Service Pilots delivered combat planes and flew test missions for the Army Air Forces, they were considered civilians and denied military benefits.

Military women, like these air transport pilots, broke down social barriers by taking on jobs that had traditionally been held only by men.

Discrimination limited opportunities for black soldiers too. Until 1942, the navy accepted black volunteers only as stewards (kitchen and laundry servants) and construction workers. The army assigned black draftees to the Army Service Forces (ASF)—the support divisions at the rear of the fighting—as truck drivers, dock workers, trash collectors, and ditch diggers. Unwelcome in the Army Air Corps before 1941, black pilots trained "as an experiment" at the Tuskegee Institute in Alabama. Like many all-black units, the Tuskegee Airmen went on to distinguish themselves in combat. But in the United States, the military gave African Americans little encouragement. In 1945, only 2 percent of all officers were black. Believing that black officers could not command respect, the army refused to place them in charge of troops in battle.

SERVICE IN THE STATES

Only one in eight Americans in uniform experienced combat during World War II. More than four million GIs never even left the United States. Their military duty included every occupation from cook to lawyer to shopkeeper to classroom instructor to psychiatrist to newspaper reporter. Like the backstage crew in a theater, servicepeople in the United States rarely got star billing. The fighting men at the front dominated the news.

But the success of the war required hard work behind the scenes. Many observers said the United States operated the "best-dressed, best-fed, best-equipped army in the world." This achievement amazed friends and enemies alike, given how unprepared the country had been in 1941. "When the men came to these training camps, they were told to march and go through close-order drill and so forth, but they had nothing to carry," explains Lee Saunders, who served as an air force officer. "They carried broomsticks and were told to make believe they were guns."

On the home front, industry hurried to manufacture the latest tools of war, from ships to bombs, from mosquito nets to life jackets. The armed forces helped design the equipment. Dieticians at the army's Subsistence Research Laboratory in Chicago, for instance, planned combat rations—nutritious meals-to-go. Equipment specialists introduced

The military teamed up with American industry to create weapons and communication devices, such as this signal lamp aboard the U.S.S. Sandlance.

the M1 steel helmet, which not only deflected bullets but also served as a shovel, wash basin, and stool. To evaluate new gear, the military conducted research. Testers in Philadelphia, for instance, collected sweat from 200 soldiers jumping up and down on rubber sacks and applied it to fabric being developed for jungle wear. Quartermasters also listened to gripes and comments from men in the field. During the war, the army improved shovels, bags, boots, weapons, and even underwear, which went from white to khaki—less noticeable when hanging out to dry.

Military medical departments conducted experiments on service-people stationed in the United States. In Charleston, South Carolina, Wave Suzie Noon, a pharmacist's mate, dispensed new sulfa (sulfanilamide) drugs to healthy human "guinea pigs" three times a day. "Of course, I'm the one who had a reaction to it," she says. "I woke up one morning and I looked kind of funny. My lip was [swollen] down to my chin." By the time she reported to the hospital after her morning chores, she had red blisters and a high fever. She recovered after a couple of weeks in bed. But a few GIs suffered permanent health problems from tests, such as those involving poisonous mustard gas.

Usually, though, stateside duty posed few hazards. Although civilian workers earned more than soldiers, the military offered good benefits. As a yeoman in a personnel office in Washington, D.C., Lee Lund earned

For many GIs, military service involved extensive schooling. These sailors study diesel mechanics at a submarine training school in New London, Connecticut.

Aviation machinists repair airplane engines in Chicago.

$21 a month—about half a week's wages for a defense plant worker. But the navy provided food, housing, and a uniform allowance, as well as medical care and even stamps. Service personnel rode free on city buses and at a discount on other public transportation.

While the government rationed (limited) supplies of butter, sugar, meat, and all sorts of luxuries for civilians during the war, soldiers could usually buy what they wanted. Waves like Lund enjoyed "ship's service, where we could get almost anything that was not available on the outside." Lund bought silk stockings for herself and cigarettes for her father. "Other than going to work and doing your job and doing it well, we had no responsibilities. No rent to worry about, no grocery bills to worry about," she says.

In return for this security, the military expected obedience. After training, recruits received active-duty assignments. Sometimes they were given a choice of positions, but transfer orders uprooted people all the time. Suzie Noon applied for a post in Hawaii, but her captain ordered her to dental corps school in Maryland.

In a sense, boot camp never ended. Unlike civilians, soldiers and sailors did not always go off duty after eight hours of work. They could not leave their bases without signing out. Often they pulled extra duties, such as standing guard all night. Wave Lee Lund recalls:

> Every Saturday they had inspections of your room and your person. Two officers would come in with their white gloves. . . and they would touch the furniture. They'd go into your closet and look at the bottom of your shoes even. . . . You had to make your bunk very tight. . . . You had to be perfect.

Still, everyone had some free time in the evenings or on Sundays. Often GIs just hung around the barracks, talking, playing cards, and writing letters. Many camps also had service clubs, with a small library, a game room, and a lounge that doubled as a ballroom. The United Service Organizations (USO) sponsored dances on Saturday nights, busing in local girls with watchful chaperones. Concerts and films played regularly on bases.

Many service personnel requested passes for town. In Washington, D.C., military men and women gathered at G Street on Wednesday, Saturday, and Sunday nights. "This sailor would go over to the piano before the dance started," Lee Lund recalls, "and he would play the 'Boogie Woogie Bugle [Boy] of Company D.'" Soldiers and sailors also blew off steam in rough entertainment districts nicknamed "Bug Town" or "The Strip." There, bars and tattoo parlors catered to restless young men, and prostitutes did a brisk business.

A CIVILIAN SALUTE

Before the attack on Pearl Harbor, soldiers and sailors had a reputation as troublemakers. Some restaurants refused to seat men in uniform. During World War II, however, public opinion changed. The massive call-up of civilians meant every family knew someone in uniform. The armed forces represented a cross section of the population, and merchants welcomed soldiers, despite sometimes rowdy behavior.

Patriotism ran high during the early 1940s, with the public united behind the war effort. Responsible for civilian cheerleading, the government's Office of War Information (OWI) encouraged the media to publicize the courage and compassion of "our boys." Certainly the war did inspire acts of incredible bravery. When a torpedo hit the troop transport ship *Dorchester* off the coast of Greenland in 1943, for instance, four chaplains aboard passed out all the life jackets, leaving none for themselves. They went down with the wreck—two Protestants, a Catholic, and a Jew—standing arm in arm. The Office of War Information made sure newspapers, magazines, radio stations, and filmmakers heard of such heroic acts. When matinee idols like John Wayne and Cary Grant carried off nearly impossible missions in war movies, everyone in uniform looked like a hero too.

Stateside service was respected, comfortable, and out of harm's way. For women especially, the advantages of military life outweighed the restrictions. By federal law, women received pay equal to that of male enlistees. (However, men's dependents—wife and children—automatically received a monthly government allowance, up to $60, while a woman

War movies, such as The Sands of Iwo Jima *starring John Wayne (*right*), helped glorify the American fighting force.*

had to prove she supported her family to earn it.) After the war, all female GIs (except Wasps) qualified for veterans' benefits.

Waves, Wacs, Spars, Wasps, and Women Marines also took pride in their role as pioneers in male institutions. They proved that women could forecast weather, instruct student gunners, fly fighter planes like the P-51 Mustang, and graduate top of the class in coed hospital corps school. "We were a sharp bunch," says Wave surgical assistant Sara McCullough. Most servicewomen delighted in the adventure as well as the work—living away from home, traveling, making friends from around the country. "Best three years of my life," says Lee Lund.

Male draftees had more mixed experiences. Some felt appreciated; others felt used. Unenthusiastic recruits, who considered their hitch in uniform only temporary, often had little respect for military traditions. This disrespect, especially for rank, irritated longtime soldiers. The

Military Police (MPs) sometimes arrested misbehaving GIs, including those on pass in town caught refusing to salute an officer. Discipline was an ongoing conflict.

Racial hostility both on and off base lowered the morale of black troops. Even in the North, MPs enforced segregation, kicking black soldiers out of base theaters or service clubs. In the South, locals threatened, beat, shot, and even hanged black GIs. Some troops rioted. In 1943,

African American soldiers—including these naval recruits—trained and served separately during World War II.

Judge William H. Hastie, an aide to the secretary of war, publicly criticized the army for not building "comradeship" in military and civilian communities:

> At Camp Stewart, Georgia, Negro soldiers and military policemen engage in a fatal gun battle. In Centerville, Mississippi, a sheriff kills a Negro soldier. At Camp Shelby, Mississippi, two Negro soldiers lie in a hospital, wounded in an affray [fight] with highway patrolmen.... Day by day the Negro soldier faces abuse and humiliation. In such a climate resentments, hatreds and fears and misunderstandings mount until they erupt in sensational violence.

White officers commanding black units rarely stood up for their men. According to George Coar, leaders bullied black troops into submission by threatening to court-martial (prosecute) them for disobedience—with penalties ranging from a prison term to death by firing squad. In a letter to the *Philadelphia Afro-American* newspaper, one GI wrote:

> In Texas, where we're not even as good as dogs, much less soldiers, our General on the post hates the sight of a colored soldier. Why, I ask you, do we have to fight on the home front for our lives then go across seas and fight again?

To prevent mutiny within the disgruntled ranks, the military had to bend. The army placed an officer in each regiment who was responsible for raising morale, and it abolished unpopular rules, such as requiring a private to get permission to marry. For the benefit of minority troops, the War Department forbade commanding officers to use racial slurs. African American celebrities, such as boxer Joe Louis, entertained on bases, and the military started accepting blood donations from blacks. Although the White House did not ban all segregation in the armed forces until 1948, army and navy officer training programs began enrolling blacks and whites together during World War II. "This was the beginning of the change," George Coar says.

WAR ACROSS THE ATLANTIC

We always tried to make the best of every situation. GIs were like that. You were there; you had a job to do; and we did it.
—Charles Ives,
army radio operator

In 1942 the German army controlled the heart of Europe. From Scandinavia in the north to Greece in the south, governments friendly to the United States had fallen to the invaders. German tank divisions had crossed the Mediterranean Sea to North Africa. Hitler's troops had also penetrated northeast from Germany into the Soviet Union.

Although Japan, operating in the Pacific, had drawn the United States into war, President Franklin D. Roosevelt (FDR) gave top priority to defeating Germany and Italy. Representing the Allies—two dozen nations opposing the Axis—FDR and British Prime Minister Winston Churchill agreed on a strategy: Stop the German advance, then force a retreat.

American forces in Europe participated in three major invasions. In 1942 Allied troops landed in the North African country of Algeria. After clearing the Germans out of Africa, the Allies invaded Sicily and nearby Italy in 1943. Meanwhile, pilots stationed in Britain pounded Hitler's strongholds from the air. Finally, Allied forces crossed the English Channel and invaded occupied France. On June 6, 1944—known as D day— American and British troops stormed the beaches of the French province of Normandy and began driving the Germans back to their borders.

Transporting millions of troops and their equipment across the Atlantic Ocean challenged the United States. Since the airline industry was in its infancy in 1941, the military hauled tanks, trucks, food, and men to Europe by ship. The government took over commercial cargo vessels. (As a result, civilians faced shortages of everything from South American coffee to Indian burlap.) Luxurious ocean liners stopped ferrying rich travelers and loaded soldiers instead. Shipyard employees in the United States worked overtime to assemble vessels called "Liberty Ships," which could hold 10,000 tons of cargo.

The ocean voyage itself could be deadly. German U-boats (submarines) prowled the Atlantic, laying explosive mines near harbors and torpedoing Allied vessels. Because of the threat of U-boats, Europe-bound ships banded together in convoys for protection. On board, GIs carried or wore life jackets at all times.

In addition to torpedo worries, crowding made for an uncomfortable crossing. On the huge liners, the army bunked men in ballrooms and stacked berths up to five high in cabins emptied of furniture. Built for about 2,500 passengers, the *Queen Mary* eventually loaded a whole division—about 16,000 men. Sometimes beds were so scarce that GIs slept in shifts—if they could sleep at all. Sailing from Virginia to Scotland on the *Aquitania*, George Coar remembers lying awake in stuffy quarters below deck as the former pleasure ship zigged and zagged to evade any U-boats hiding in the sea.

At least ocean liners crossed with speed. The *Aquitania*, for instance, docked within a week. On a cargo-laden Liberty Ship, which held only 550 troops with gear, Bill Folley's ride from Virginia to Italy took 32 days. For many landlubber troops like Folley, the voyage was "sea-sickening." Some days men felt too ill to stand, let alone report to the deck to exercise. Limited water and nasty food compounded the misery. A mechanic with a bomber squadron, Folley recalls:

> We had breakfast, which was terrible, and lunch, which was worse.... There were little white worms floating around in [the oatmeal]. I complained to the doctor, and he said, "Oh, it's okay—they're cooked." And I said, "They're not cooked done; they're still moving."

Fortunately, most GIs did not step off a boat and into battle. While they regained their land legs, they faced another dizzying experience: culture shock. Many draftees had never left the United States—or even their home states—before. They understood only English. To ask directions or buy snacks, they now had to communicate with people who spoke Arabic, Italian, or French. War Department booklets explained the customs of foreign countries and instructed troops how not to offend natives. For example, GIs headed for Arab North Africa were warned not to touch or stare at women in veils: "Serious injury if not death at the hands of Moslem men may result." In Britain, Americans felt more at home, even if they had to flip to pocket guides to translate words such as

GIs chat with civilians in an English town.

Troops rush into the fighting at Wernberg, Germany.

lift (elevator) and *first floor* (second floor). "The British don't know how to make a good cup of coffee," said one book. "You don't know how to make a good cup of tea. It's an even swap."

Americans endeared themselves to shopkeepers everywhere, though. They earned more than other Allied troops, and the Army boosted a soldier's pay by 10 percent when he arrived overseas. Yet free-spending GIs also annoyed their hosts. They drank excessively and bragged loudly. Americans also bought up scarce food and flirted with local girls at restaurants and nightclubs. As the British often complained, "The trouble with you Yanks is that you're overpaid, oversexed, and over here."

UNDER THE GUN

Neither boot camp nor booklets could prepare soldiers for the front lines, though. Battle required hard labor, attention to detail, and mental stamina. Everyone had to perform a job under the most stressful conditions. As GIs often remarked, no one gets used to combat.

After landing in Italy, Bill Folley's bombing group camped in an olive grove within earshot of enemy fire. At first they slept in pup tents. Later they moved into four-man pyramid tents, which were warmed with homemade stoves—oil barrels filled with sand and heated with burning diesel fuel. The bathroom was a 16-hole outhouse.

On rainy days, the makeshift airport turned to mud. To prepare the huge B-24 bombers for takeoff, ground crews had to pull the planes onto solid ground with tractors. Before the flight crews boarded, at any hour of the day or night, mechanics checked the aircraft and cleared them for flight.

The bombers took off for missions in Italy, Austria, and Germany. Many were shot down. Folley remembers:

> Sometimes maybe ten airplanes would start out, and you'd only have six when they came back, or four. Eventually you'd hear that some of [your friends] were prisoners. Some of them would come back later on. You never knew. So you had to keep up the faith.

When returning with wounded, the B-24s turned on their landing lights or launched a red flare. An ambulance and fire trucks waited at the end of the runway. As soon as the plane had emptied, the maintenance mechanics assessed the damage. Repairs could be grim. "When the gunner up here in the nose would be hit . . . about all that would be left would be blood and guts," says Folley, a technical sergeant later promoted to crew chief. "They'd wash it down with a fire hose, and they'd have to replace the turret."

Unlike the air corps, the ground forces didn't return to a base after each mission. Infantrymen fought on the move. Often engineering units cleared the way, building or repairing roads and disabling mines. Although jeeps and trucks carried equipment, the average soldier walked, toting his backpack. One misty morning, mortar battalion radio operator Charles Ives climbed down a hill with about 100 pounds of gear, including a 38-pound radio and a 20-pound belt of ammunition:

> Every time fire would come in, we'd hit the ground. Well, I hit the ground, and the radio would come up and conk me in the head. . . . I was groggy. I couldn't even get up a couple of times.

An infantry regiment marches along a snow-covered road in Belgium.

Infantrymen earned the nickname "blisterfoot." General George Patton figured that his Third Army crossed 24 major rivers, passed through 1,500 towns, and liberated 82,000 square miles of territory in 281 days of combat after D day. Many Americans suffered from a condition called trench foot (which made feet swell and blister) from wearing wet shoes and leggings for long periods at a time. In *Up Front* (1945), Bill Mauldin described the suffering of the "dogfaces" (another nickname for GIs) pinned down by fire for days or weeks at a time in soggy foxholes and trenches:

> If they couldn't stand the pain, they crawled out of their holes... down the mountain until they reached the aid station. Their shoes were cut off, and their feet swelled like balloons. Sometimes the feet had to be amputated. But most often the men had to make their agonized way back up the mountain.

To keep troops mobile and healthy, the army began to insist on a daily sock exchange (take off the wet, put on the dry). Quartermasters soon replaced canvas leggings and shoes with hightop leather combat boots or rubber-bottomed moccasins.

Far behind the front lines, generals planned strategy. They radioed their orders to commanders in the field. On paper, war looked simple. Planes bombed enemy positions. Mortar and artillery battalions lobbed shells over their frontline troops to "soften up" the opposition. Then tanks and infantrymen advanced firing.

But in reality, combat was tricky. The enemy was shifting and shooting back. Rain turned hillsides into slippery slopes. Fog cut off a scout's view through binoculars. Firing weapons threw up noise and smoke. Officers shouted orders; wounded men screamed with pain. Battle verged on chaos.

"I was proud to be an American, and a soldier as far as that goes," says Charles Ives. "But . . . a combat situation is never where you want to be."

During an assault, troops rarely had time or energy to set up camp. At night, under cover of darkness, the Army Service Forces carried

Foot soldiers line up for a hot meal. More often, GIs on the move ate cold rations.

ammunition, water, dry socks, batteries, and food to the front—by jeep, foot, or even mule. Although kitchens on trucks sometimes provided hot meals, GIs often dined on field rations: portable meals consisting of a main dish, biscuits, and extras like dried fruit, instant coffee, candy, cigarettes, and gum. Individual C-rations came in tiny gold cans (which were later painted green to prevent enemy pilots from charting a division's path from the shiny litter soldiers left on the ground). Boxed K-rations provided 3,400 calories a day, but few soldiers could stomach the whole menu. According to Ives:

> The C-rations were much better than the K-rations. The K-rations were like eating dog food.... At least we had a variety [in C-rations]. You have corned beef; you have beans; you have spaghetti.

On evenings when they could build a fire without drawing German shells, troops warmed up the canned dishes for a "gourmet" meal.

Soldiers in motorized divisions sometimes carried tents or slept in bedrolls in trucks. But many servicemen just collapsed on a blanket on the ground or in a hole, with their pack for a pillow. In the artillery in Europe, Bob Baldridge recalls:

> Normally you did sleep at night. But you learned to take cat-naps during the day, 'cause you'd be pulling guard duty or be involved in firing missions during the night. I got so I could sleep during the daytime when we were moving, riding along in a bumpy jeep.

In winter, even in wool trousers, GIs woke up chilled to the bone—or worse, numb with frostbite.

Sometimes soldiers dug latrines. Often they just headed into the woods with their daily ration of 22½ sheets of toilet paper. In Normandy, Charles Ives's unit spent 35 straight days in combat. "Never had a change of clothes, never had a chance to take a bath, nothing," he says.

The hardships often blurred the distinctions between officers and enlisted men. So too did "battlefield commissions," when commanders promoted "one of the guys" to officer. While serving in Europe from

1943 to 1945, Bob Baldridge rose in rank from private to second lieutenant. He recalls:

> The officers and the men were separate in times of peace. Officers had different living quarters than the men. But in combat, everybody slept on the ground. . . . In combat, everybody's together. You shared things. . . . There was no problem unless one guy one way or the other was a real jerk, which could happen.

In the field, jerks ran into problems. A careless officer risked the lives of all the men he led. On rare occasions, soldiers would mutiny, disobeying or even shooting a distrusted commander. More likely, he would get himself into trouble. The white captain of George Coar's all-black tank destroyer unit thought himself a mine expert. But he blew himself up by stepping into a booby-trapped crater. "When he was killed, there was a celebration," Coar says. He was "one of the worst racists I think there ever was."

Combat, although horrifying at times, forged a sense of unity among GIs.

REST AND RELAXATION

Even near the front, soldiers found ways to relax. They played cards in foxholes. They told jokes. One popular army joke described a lieutenant who scolded an infantryman with a bullet in his leg: "Don't just lie there," the lieutenant said. "Do push-ups until an ambulance gets here!" As Bill Mauldin observed in *Up Front,*

> The infantrymen can't live without friends...and that's the reason men at the front seem so much simpler and more generous than others. They kid each other unmercifully.

During lulls at Bill Folley's bomber base in Italy, the pilots flew the planes to the chilly air at high altitudes to cool beer or to make ice cream.

Often GIs joked about easy jobs in the Army Service Forces: one man on the front line and five to carry up the Coca-Cola. The actual combat-to-ASF ratio was closer to one to three, and kidding aside, the men and women of the ASF did much more than transport soft drinks to troops in combat. Besides keeping medical care and supplies right behind the soldiers, special ASF trucks doubled as recreation vehicles, carrying everything from baseballs to drums to theatrical makeup for army shows.

With military aid, the Red Cross (an international relief agency based in Switzerland) and the USO also traveled to the front to pass out doughnuts or provide entertainment. Sometimes Hollywood stars performed in battle zones, but more often the talent was local. "We had girls dancing on the truck one day," says Charles Ives, "and shells started to come pretty close. We said, 'Well, ladies, we had better go.'"

The army distributed free stress relievers such as cigarettes and gum. It also delivered *Stars & Stripes,* an official army newspaper printed in Europe. "It was humorous and also put the best light on everything," says Bob Baldridge. "And we knew that."

For a more honest assessment of the war, troops subscribed to magazines. The military put tremendous effort into delivering mail. During combat, mail might not catch up to a unit for several weeks, but when it

Mail call draws an eager crowd aboard a Coast Guard ship.

did, "it was great for your morale," says Bob Baldridge. "You'd pass around three-week-old and five-week-old magazines." Packages arrived too. "We wanted food and special equipment like better gloves in the wintertime or more undershirts.... Whenever you got a box of food, you'd normally split it up with your friends." Bill Folley recalls that several of his buddies had been raised on farms, so their parents sent homegrown popcorn. In the evening, the plane mechanics sat around building ham radios, eating popcorn, and drinking Italian wine.

The most important deliveries were letters. As army Lieutenant Charles Taylor wrote to his wife in 1944:

> After a while, you more or less become numb from being homesick and then you get a real good letter and all the time you are reading the letter, your mind is back home and you see nothing around you. A letter is truly a "ten-minute" furlough [vacation], as is said by the men.

Mail didn't always bring happy news. Soldiers dreaded a "Dear John" letter from a wife or girlfriend who had fallen in love with another man. But usually civilians on the home front took care to send cheer and support. Wives enclosed pictures of babies. Parents forwarded the local newspaper. The words of encouragement reminded Americans why they were fighting.

Even GIs who acted tough and cool in front of their buddies often confided their hopes and fears in letters home. Correspondence drew many couples closer together. Bill Folley wrote his friend BettyLou Kanton every other day—almost 350 letters in all—and after the war, they married. In combat, a GI was not supposed to keep a diary, lest it fall into enemy hands. Some Americans broke the rule, but most used the mail as a sort of journal. In letters to his wife, Charles Taylor grappled with one of the heaviest burdens of combat—shooting another human being:

> You know, it's all like a big game, but it is bad to kill, I guess. At first, I did a lot of worrying, but I guess I got used to it.... I hope God will not hold anything against me.

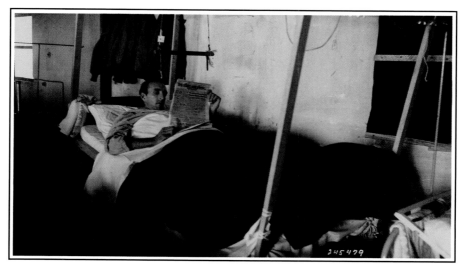

An injured GI catches up on war news with Stars & Stripes.

WAR ACROSS THE PACIFIC

*The only way you could get it over
with was to kill them off before they
killed you. The war I knew was
totally savage.*
　　　—Marine E. B. Sledge
　　　in *"The Good War"*

The Japanese attack on Pearl Harbor in 1941 crippled the American Pacific Fleet. As the United States reeled from that blow, Japanese forces swept across the Pacific. The Imperial Army overran American outposts on Guam and Wake Island and drove the British out of Hong Kong and Malaya. Next fell Borneo and the Dutch East Indies. More than 16,000 U.S. troops stationed in the Philippines tried to repel an invasion, but the Japanese drove them back to the Bataan peninsula and the island of Corregidor.

With not enough ships or soldiers available to rush reinforcements to the far Pacific, President Roosevelt ordered General Douglas MacArthur to retreat from the Philippines to Australia. "I shall return," MacArthur promised. He left behind thousands of Americans and Filipinos, who surrendered in the spring of 1942 and became prisoners of war.

"Our country was so unprepared," says Lou Curtis. A musician, he joined the Marine Corps in 1939 and played saxophone in embassy and regimental bands in Peking and Shanghai, China. In November 1941, his unit shipped out for the Philippines. War surprised them. Trapped on Corregidor, they held out as long as possible:

> We had the ability to fight . . . but if you don't have equipment, you don't have food, you can't do it on spirit. . . . This country was concentrated on Europe at the time. . . . We sure did feel left out.

The Allies did not abandon the Pacific front, however. In the 1942 Battle of Midway, outnumbered American naval forces destroyed four Japanese aircraft carriers and more than 300 airplanes—evening the score after Pearl Harbor. For the rest of the war, the Allies took the offensive.

Thanks to its industrial might, the United States was able to rebuild its fleet quickly. Between 1942 and 1944, American shipyards turned out 14 enormous aircraft carriers—ships with flat decks that served as airplane runways.

American and Australian troops drove the Japanese from the jungly Solomon Islands, then from the flat coral islands of Micronesia. By 1945 the Allies had reclaimed the Philippines and secured the Mariana Islands, Okinawa, and Iwo Jima. From there, B-29 bombers took off to rain fire bombs on Japanese cities. With a German surrender likely, the United States planned to transfer troops from Europe to the Pacific for an all-out invasion of Japan.

ISLAND BY ISLAND

There were similarities between combat in Europe and combat in the Pacific. First, troops had to travel across an ocean to reach the front. Liberty Ships and converted ocean liners ferried troops from the mainland to Hawaii and then on to Australia or an island base such as New Guinea. There, Americans had to adjust to the odd customs of their allies. Australians, known as "Aussies," called pals "mates." New Guinea

Marines take a cigarette break on a bleak Peleliu Island battlefield.

tribesmen wore face paint and feathered headdresses. With cigarettes, soap, or American money, soldiers and sailors could buy comforts and souvenirs—from laundry service to pet kangaroos. Foreigners often found Americans spoiled but also admired their enthusiasm.

Thousands of sailors lived and worked on "task forces"—an aircraft carrier (sometimes several) surrounded by battleships, cruisers, and destroyers. These floating battle groups could stay at sea on a mission for more than two months. The great distances in the Pacific did not stop official efforts to keep troops contented. About every four days, a "sea train" of oil tankers and supply ships arrived with fuel, fresh vegetables, mail, and movies. Navy vessels also brought supplies to island bases, even dropping off USO entertainers now and then.

Still, GIs felt isolated on islands and at sea. In Europe the army often passed near populated areas. In the Pacific, hungry infantrymen rarely saw a farmhouse door to knock on. Lonely marines couldn't sneak off to a local pub to order a beer or meet a woman. The navy prohibited alcohol aboard ship. Fewer GIs went AWOL (absent without leave) in the Pacific because they had nowhere to go. "There were none of the European diversions," army clerk Robert Lekachman recalled in *"The Good War."* "What you tended to see were miserable natives and piles of dead Japanese and dead Americans."

Fighting differed too. Amphibious (sea to land) assaults like D day were important in Europe, but few. Once landed, troops continued through Europe on foot. In the Pacific, marines and infantrymen stormed beaches on a regular basis. Typically, battleship crews pounded island defenses with their heavy guns and tried to hit airfields to keep Japanese planes from taking off. Next, Allied pilots flying from carriers or nearby bases inflicted more damage with bombs and bullets. Then amphibious vehicles slid from ships through the water and onto beaches to unload men, jeeps, bulldozers, and tanks. Sometimes paratroopers jumped behind enemy lines.

Finally GIs advanced, firing flamethrowers and tossing grenades. On most of the islands, Japanese soldiers had dug themselves into hillside caves or "pillboxes"—little forts of concrete, coral, palm logs, and steel beams. There they waited with rifles cocked, ready to shoot an exposed target.

If Allied tanks were able to climb the muddy slopes or penetrate the undergrowth, they blasted the pillboxes. Sometimes bulldozers buried the enemy alive. More often men fought with machine guns and rifles at short range—and at great human cost. In a 1945 article for *Yank*, Sergeant Bill Reed described the landing on Iwo Jima, where enemy machine guns and mortars at the foot of a volcano pinned marines down in the sand for two days:

> The sight of a head raised above a foxhole was the signal to dozens of [Japanese], safely hidden in concrete emplacements, to open up. Men lay on their sides to drink from canteens or to urinate.... Bad weather and a choppy ocean held up the supply of new ammunition and equipment and evacuation of the wounded.

Antiaircraft gunners in action aboard the carrier U.S.S. Hornet

Navigators guide the U.S.S. Lexington into enemy waters during a 1943 strike on the Gilbert and Marshall islands.

In a month-long battle on tiny Peleliu Island in September 1944, Japanese soldiers in caves put up so much resistance that Americans called the battleground Bloody Nose Ridge. About 11,000 Japanese and 1,800 Americans died in the fighting, and another 8,000 GIs were wounded.

Although troops in Europe struggled with mud and cold, at least the countryside reminded them of places back in the States—pine forests, grassy pastures, river valleys. The Pacific presented alien landscapes— steamy jungles and ragged atolls (coral islands). Dense vegetation offered some cover during an attack, but the jungle spooked Americans. Crocodiles and snakes slithered into swamps. At night, creatures made strange noises. Troops had to hack through vines and scrub, and men and machines often sank deep into the ooze created by heavy afternoon rains.

According to Marine Robert Leckie in *Strong Men Armed,* the hot and humid jungle bred "spiders as big as your fist and wasps as long as your finger...tree-leeches...scorpions...centipedes whose foul scurrying leaves a track of inflamed flesh." Maggots and ants swarmed over the dead. Bugs spread diseases too. In the sharp, head-high kunai grass,

The tropical landscapes of southeast Asia were unsettling to American troops, most of whom had never traveled far from home.

biting mites transmitted scrub typhus. Flies landed on food, spreading dysentery, and infected troops lost weight through severe diarrhea. Mosquitoes carried malaria and dengue fever (which causes severe pain in the joints).

Once Allied fighters had gained the upper hand after an invasion, the navy's construction battalions—Seabees—began transforming the mess into home. Like most military subdivisions, the Seabees had an emblem: a bee with tattooed arms buzzing around with a tommy gun, a wrench, and a hammer. By reputation, Seabees could make almost everything out of almost nothing. Within days, they erected bases on desolate islands complete with barracks, hospitals, pipelines, and underground electrical cables (to protect them from bombing). To build an airfield, they blew up tree stumps, bulldozed the earth flat, then laid Marston mat—a sort of steel carpet—as a runway. They paved highways with coral, repaired truck mufflers with worn-out bazookas, and even resoled shoes with old tires. On Guadalcanal, they turned abandoned Japanese junk into an ice machine. Marines joked that when they reached heaven, they'd find roads built by Seabees.

AN ALIEN FOE

Troops on the Atlantic and Pacific fronts felt differently about the enemies they faced. As George Coar explains, GIs had no love for Hitler or the Germans. They especially disliked Hitler's elite SS troops, who belonged to the Nazi party and declared themselves part of a "master race." Yet the Allies shared with the Germans a Western view of warfare. They respected each other's military tactics and fought by the same rules much of the time. Troops who surrendered, for instance, usually received humane treatment. Sometimes both sides would observe a temporary cease-fire so medics could rescue the wounded. Like most Americans, Bob Baldridge didn't hate Germans as individuals. He believed they just followed the wrong leader. "I never met a German—and I met plenty of them—who admitted being a Nazi. . . . I just thought they were all a bunch of jerks for allowing themselves to be taken in by Hitler and his Nazi party."

Military photographers wade through a river in a New Guinea jungle.

But Japanese culture was very foreign to Americans. As Marine E. B. Sledge told Studs Terkel in *"The Good War"*:

> The Japanese fought by a code they thought was right: *bushido*. The code of the warrior: no surrender. You don't really comprehend it until you get out there and fight people who are faced with an absolutely hopeless situation and will not give up. If you tried to help one of the Japanese, he'd usually detonate a grenade and kill himself as well as you. To be captured was a disgrace. . . . You developed an attitude of no mercy because they had no mercy on us.

Americans accused the "Japs" of not fighting fairly. Sometimes enemy troops used a wounded GI as bait, torturing him until his screams drew his pals within range of Japanese machine-gun fire. At night Japanese snipers snuck out of their pillboxes and crossed into Allied territory. American troops in foxholes slept uneasily with knives in hand. Instead of admiring Japanese jungle savvy the way they admired German artillery, GIs called Japanese soldiers cruel as well as crafty.

Fierce fighting on Iwo Jima, where more than 6,000 Americans died

Racism also shaped these attitudes. Many Americans of European descent considered Asians inferior. Edgy, angry, and afraid, troops in the Pacific often lost control of themselves. As Marine Sledge told Terkel:

> I've seen guys shoot Japanese wounded when it really was not necessary and knock gold teeth out of their mouths. . . . The way you extracted gold teeth was by putting the tip of the blade on the tooth of the dead Japanese—I've seen guys do it to wounded ones—and hit the hilt of the knife to knock the tooth loose. How could American boys do this? If you're reduced to savagery by a situation, anything's possible.

Fighting under these conditions hardened some troops and horrified others. But even in the Pacific, decency—almost a comradeship—sometimes prevailed. Once in a while, stray Japanese soldiers snuck into an American chow line on an island or into the back row during the screening of a movie. Wave Lee Lund recalls a story her husband told her. He had wounded a Japanese soldier by shooting him in the leg:

> [My husband] took his bayonet, and he was going to kill him. And the Japanese hollered, "Please don't kill me," in perfect English. My husband was so stunned. [The Japanese] said, "I have a wife and four children." He took [out] a photograph and he showed [my husband]. And my husband said, "Okay, I'll take you in as a prisoner of war."

DEATH AND OTHER FATES

It's a big, big war, and I am such
a small person in it.
*—*Army Lieutenant Charles
Taylor, letter home, 1945

Military personnel in a combat zone awoke each morning wondering if they would survive the day. Although the United States suffered fewer casualties than other Allied countries, World War II claimed the lives of more than 300,000 Americans. Infantrymen ran the highest risk of falling in battle, especially during the last 14 months of fierce fighting. Yet mines, shrapnel, bullets, torpedoes, and bombs could strike anyone at any time—even behind the front lines. Lighted and marked with a giant red cross, field hospitals and hospital ships were not supposed to come under enemy fire. But they did. Roughly 200 army nurses, all women, died in the line of duty.

Sometimes quick thinking saved a soldier. More often luck determined who would live and who would die. Charles Ives and his outfit were burying ammunition one day when a railroad gun 11 miles away began shelling them. One shell landed short. The second arched over their heads. The Americans knew another shell was coming. Five soldiers ran for a crater left over from an earlier bombing, while Ives and a friend crouched in a small hole:

> [My friend] started to get up, and I said, "You can't make it," and grabbed him by the belt and pulled him back. That shell landed right in that place where the five men were. Oh, God, that was terrible....

Whole companies occasionally perished together. More than 1,000 Americans died retaking the Pacific atoll of Tarawa from the Japanese in 1943. The assault lasted only 75 hours, but one marine battalion lost half its men.

A grave marker erected by a French civilian for an American soldier reads: "Died for France."

Some soldiers were so frightened that they couldn't function in combat. The Germans tried to fan this fear by dropping leaflets from airplanes. One showed a sexy woman with the caption "Longing for You." But when a GI flipped the leaflet over, he saw a skull. According to Ives, most Americans just laughed at these messages.

Yet GIs also wrestled with dread. George Coar was afraid the Germans would blast his unit with a poisonous chemical called white phosphorus. "That was a horrible, horrible thing to think of, something that won't go out hitting your body and burning right in." Like many troops, he found strength in religion. "I prayed a lot," he says.

Many soldiers and sailors prepared to die. Before they left the United States, GIs were instructed to write wills. The government also provided each serviceperson with a $10,000 life insurance policy. Men in combat often kept a farewell letter for their family among their possessions.

Charles Ives made his peace with death while waiting at anchor off the coast of France during the D-day invasion. A freak storm had wiped out the landing areas for his mortar battalion's trucks and jeeps, and they had to be rebuilt. The Germans were shelling the beach, dead bodies floated by in the water now and then, and his ship was running out of food—even the awful British canned liver. He dealt with the stress as so many other troops did, by taking one day at a time:

> If it was a nice day, we got out and enjoyed the sunshine. You can't be worrying all the time. You've got to live life, every day that you've got, every minute that you've got.

Death ended a soldier's worries for good, but others had to deal with the loss. The War Department sent a telegram to inform the GI's family. A general usually mailed a letter of sympathy, as did the company officer or chaplain who knew the circumstances of the soldier's death. The military also boxed up and shipped home personal gear. Rarely did GIs write to the family of a buddy who had died in battle. "You didn't know what to say," explains Bob Baldridge.

The U.S. military took pains to recover bodies. After battles, members of the Army Graves Registration Service swept the terrain. To find

Sailors killed on the aircraft carrier Liscome Bay—*which was torpedoed by the Japanese in the Gilbert Islands—are buried at sea.*

airmen lost in a plane crash, they interviewed residents near the wreckage. On Pacific islands, they dug into pillboxes. To identify GIs who had lost their dog tags, the crew used fingerprints, dental records, and even class rings as clues. Although gruesome work, treating the dead as human beings instead of numbers comforted soldiers and the families of those who had died.

Sometimes the military shipped bodies straight home. More often it buried them temporarily, with one dog tag on the body and another on the grave marker. Later, after the war, families could choose to have a soldier's remains sent home or placed in one of 14 overseas cemeteries. Locating dead Americans proved easier in Europe than in the Pacific, because the Allies and the Germans observed each other's burial customs. In the Pacific, the Japanese often cremated (burned) corpses, and the Americans bulldozed enemy dead into ditches. Sailors were buried at sea—weighted down, wrapped in canvas, and slid over the side of the ship.

BATTLE SCARS

During World War II, more than 600,000 American military men and women were injured—scratched, burned, or pierced by fragments of metal shell so hot they raised blisters from under the skin. Half joking, GIs hoped for a "million-dollar wound": serious enough to remove them from the front lines but harmless enough to spare them permanent disability. "The trouble with that is, they usually came back within six to eight months," Bob Baldridge observes. "But [by then] the average soldier wanted to get back to his unit." As GIs recovered, they often felt guilty about not sharing battlefield danger with their buddies. Almost three out of every four wounded soldiers eventually returned to duty.

The faster a wounded serviceman received treatment, the better his chances for survival. Everyone carried a first-aid kit. In training, troops had learned to stop bleeding by applying pressure with bandages or tourniquets. Usually though, an injured GI, in shock and in pain, counted on medics for first aid. Unarmed, medical corpsmen wore a red cross on their uniforms. But the red cross didn't stop enemy fire, and sometimes hours passed before medics could rescue a man. Some medics were con-scientious objectors (men opposed to war on religious or ethical grounds) who refused to bear arms. As Bill Mauldin wrote in *Up Front* (1945), the medic's courage impressed troops:

> The dogface's real hero is the litter bearer and the aid man who goes into all combat situations right along with the in-fantryman, shares his hardships and dangers, and isn't able to fight back. When the infantryman is down, the medic must get up and help him. That's not pleasant sometimes when there's shooting.

Wounded men walked or were carried to a battalion aid station—just "the surgeon's medical chest and a few stretchers under a tree," accord-ing to newspaper reporter Ernie Pyle. In the army, roughly 26 percent of infantrymen suffered injuries, and about 96 percent of those wounded men who reached an aid station survived their injuries. At the aid station, a doctor and about three dozen corpsmen stabilized each patient. They gave morphine to ease pain, transfused blood plasma to reduce shock, patched life-threatening wounds, and administered penicillin or sprinkled sulfa powder to prevent infection.

Then the injured soldiers began a long journey by stretcher, jeep, truck, ambulance, or even ship to a full-service hospital in safe territory. Along the way, they stopped for treatment at field hospitals or clinics.

In Italy *Life* magazine photographer Margaret Bourke-White watched a nurse at a Fifth Army field hospital give a blood tranfusion to a young man who had lost both legs. Since German artillery had knocked out

Medics assist a fellow medic wounded on a French battlefield.

the hospital's electrical generator, Bourke-White remembers, the nurse worked by flashlight. Whenever a round of enemy fire whistled in, she hit the floor. "As soon as we heard the bang of the exploding shell, the nurse was back on her feet checking those transfusion needles," Bourke-White wrote in her autobiography. That nurse, a Texan, told the photographer that doctors called her every time they received a patient from Texas. "It seems to help the boys to know someone from their own home state is taking care of them," the nurse said.

Battle hurt servicemen psychologically as well as physically. As many as 500,000 GIs suffered "combat fatigue" or got "nervous in the service." Many men had nightmares. Some acted like zombies, going through the motions of fighting in a trance. Others raged, snapping at their friends and suspecting faithful wives back home of betrayal. A few soldiers who couldn't stand the strain shot their own feet, hoping to be sent back to the United States. More developed "battlefield fever": aches

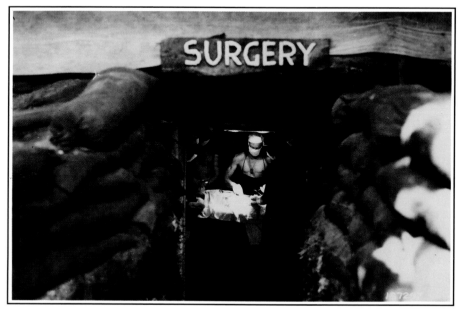

Some medical facilities, like this underground operating room, were makeshift shelters not far from the front line.

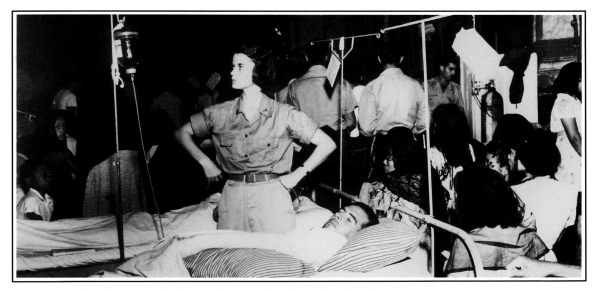

In this evacuation hospital, set up in a Filipino church, an American nurse monitors GI patients alongside churchgoers at a Christmas Eve worship service.

and a high temperature of no known origin. As Ernie Pyle wrote in *Brave Men* (1944):

> The doctors thought it was caused by a combination of too much dust, bad eating, not enough sleep, exhaustion, and the unconscious nerve tension that comes to everybody in a frontline area. A man doesn't die of battlefield fever, but he thinks he's going to.

Although some officers considered combat fatigue cowardice, the military as a whole treated it as an illness. Usually, a short rest in a hospital to the rear relieved the worst symptoms, but some GIs needed prolonged psychiatric care. In 1944 the army began to arrange monthlong furloughs (time off) for some frontline veterans. But manpower was in such short supply that not many soldiers could take a vacation from combat.

Late draftees—fathers, teens, factory workers without deferments— filled the empty slots left by casualties. Joining veterans, replacements often felt alone and ill at ease. Whole companies—hastily trained and shipped overseas after the D-day invasion—often suffered from poor morale, as Bob Baldridge recalls:

> New units, the untrained divisions, where the soldiers hadn't worked together for a long time, they were the ones with problems, such as avoiding real duty, shooting themselves in the foot, getting trench foot in the winter because they didn't know how to handle it.

The replacement system had one unexpected side effect: integration. By the end of the war, commanders assigned individual black troops to fill out white infantry units.

BEHIND BARBED WIRE

More than 120,000 Americans ended up as prisoners of war (POWs) during World War II. Sometimes generals in a hopeless situation negotiated a large-scale surrender, as at Bataan and Corregidor in the Philippines. Usually though, soldiers gave up individually or in small groups. Patrols were lost or trapped behind enemy lines. Crews in disabled planes crash-landed and were captured.

On the whole, Americans treated their POWs well. In transit to Allied territory, prisoners ate C-rations. Shipped back to the United States, they lived and worked in camps. In Stark, New Hampshire, for instance, they chopped wood. At Fort Knox in Kentucky, a German POW oompah band entertained American officers.

But stories of German maltreatment of American POWs brought out a desire for revenge. After the bloody Battle of the Bulge in Belgium in December 1944, George Coar saw many Americans "who had been captured and tortured." The Nazi SS troops had a hateful reputation. Coar heard:

> A group of white GIs were captured, and they were put out there at this intersection to be counted, so they thought. SS troops just turned their machine guns on them and mowed them down.... There was a feeling under no circumstances would we take prisoner an SS trooper. He had to die.

A line of Americans captured after a surprise German attack near the western front.

The Bataan "Death March." Americans and Filipinos carry their comrades who have fallen en route to the Cabanatuan prison camp.

In general, Allied POWs fared better under the Germans than under the Japanese. The Germans had set up a prison system, with separate camps for officers. Conditions varied widely. Some camps had hot showers; others had holes in the floor for latrines. In accordance with the 1929 Geneva Convention, at which governments had set guidelines for the treatment of prisoners of war, some Nazi officers paid POWs for their work and cooperated with the Red Cross. Although the Germans fed prisoners mostly black bread and potatoes, they allowed Red Cross medical supplies and food parcels, as well as mail from home, to reach prisoners regularly.

The Japanese, on the other hand, did not work closely with the Red Cross. While the average POW in Germany lost 38 pounds during captivity, the average prisoner of the Japanese lost 61 pounds. At the beginning of the war, the Imperial Army captured thousands of Americans, but it didn't have an organized plan for how to keep them. During the infamous Bataan "Death March" in 1942, thousands of Americans and Filipinos died of starvation, disease, and exhaustion on the way to the Cabanatuan prison camp.

Marine Lou Curtis was one of 5,000 Americans who surrendered on Corregidor in May 1942. "I don't think the Japanese were prepared for so many men," he says. Split into groups and loaded into barges, the POWs traveled to Manila, then on to Cabanatuan. "I remember being put in a boxcar and the terrible things that went on there, people passing out from heat exhaustion, no water." So many men were starving at Cabanatuan that Curtis and some buddies volunteered for a work detail in the hope of getting fed.

For the next two years, Curtis lived in a Japanese camp on the Philippine island of Palawan. The POWs were supposed to be building an airstrip, but "we did as much sabotage as we could," says Curtis. "We didn't mix the cement right. Actually, when the Japanese planes landed on [the runways], a lot cracked up."

Curtis and his pals didn't mind the hard labor because it afforded them an opportunity to supplement their meager diet of rice. "We all weighed around 100, 115 pounds," he says. "While we were in the jungle, we'd steal coconuts, steal bananas and papayas. They tried to catch us, but we got pretty good at stealing."

Disobedience was dangerous, however. Curtis remembers that the Japanese beheaded two men who tried to escape. "The older Japanese might not be so severe, but the young Japanese, they treated us brutal," Curtis says. "Some of them would look for any excuse to beat us."

The Japanese often delayed notifying the Red Cross of the names of POWs. Families in the United States knew only that a man was missing in action. Once Lou Curtis's sister learned of his fate, she mailed him a recorder, a substitute for his beloved saxophone. Although the Japanese distributed mail and food parcels haphazardly, Lou Curtis received his little flute—a year and a half after his capture.

"I played marches and everything on that," he says. "We had a guy make a guitar out of a box and a set of drums. . . . Every prison camp had

IMPERIAL JAPANESE ARMY

1. I am interned at—Philippine Military Prison Camp No. _le-A._

2. My health is—excellent; good; fair; poor.

3. Message (50 words limit)

Dear Mary- Merry Xmas and a Happy New Year.

Hope you are well and happy. I'm doing as well as

can be expected under these conditions. Give my

regards to all.

_____

Louis Newton Curtis
Signature

Top: *Red Cross workers prepare Christmas gift boxes to be shipped to American servicemen.* Bottom: *A postcard home from Lou Curtis, imprisoned in the Philippines*

a bunch of guys get together, make their own instruments, get a little band going." The music cheered up everyone. "The Japs used to listen to it. They liked it. In fact, some of the better Japs used to give us a little extra rice."

The Imperial Army allowed GIs to send postcards limited to 50 words. On one Curtis thanked his sister for the gift and urged her to keep the faith. "My prayer is: You will not lose courage under any condition," he wrote.

Like most GIs, Curtis didn't doubt the Allies were going to win the war, so he just tried to hang on. Rumors of U.S. victories reached POW camps. With most of the construction finished on Palawan in the fall of 1944, the camp commander divided the prisoners. Curtis and a group of 150 POWs travelled to Manila and then joined other prisoners on the way to Japan. The trip by sea—in the hot, crowded, unsanitary holds of "Hell Ships"—killed many malnourished men. The GIs cheered when they heard U.S. planes overhead. But friendly fire sometimes brought death as well as hope when Allies unknowingly torpedoed ships or bombed trains that carried POWs.

In Japan Curtis learned just how far his luck had carried him. With American forces closing in on Palawan, the Japanese had massacred almost all of the remaining POWs—all the friends he'd left behind. "Sometimes I think, 'Why me?'" Lou Curtis says. "We all got kind of religious.... I just played it day by day.... We knew it wasn't going to last forever."

THE ROAD TO VICTORY

Home alive in '45
Out of the sticks in '46
From hell to heaven in '47
          —GI rhymes, 1940s

By mid-1944, the Allies smelled victory. In Europe they had chased the German army up the Italian peninsula, taking Rome and Florence. American and British armored divisions rooted out the enemy in France and Belgium on their way to the Rhine River. In the east, the Soviet Union, which had joined the Allies, controlled Finland, Poland, and the Baltic states. By March 1945, the Allies had marched well into Germany.

An ailing President Franklin Roosevelt died in April 1945, missing the triumph for which he had campaigned so hard. Two weeks later, Adolf Hitler committed suicide and Germany surrendered. On May 8, 1945, GIs all over the world celebrated V-E Day, Victory in Europe.

In the Pacific, the Allies also made steady progress. By October 1944, General MacArthur had returned as promised to the Philippines. After V-E Day, the United States and Britain bombarded Japan by air and by sea, a prelude to an invasion. When Japan ignored verbal and written warnings to surrender, President Harry Truman ordered the air forces to drop a new superweapon, the atomic bomb, on the Japanese port city of Hiroshima. The explosion on August 6, 1945—equal in power to 20,000 tons of dynamite—killed or injured almost 130,000 people. Three days later, a second atomic bomb ravaged Nagasaki, Japan.

Years later some Americans questioned the decision to release the destructive powers of the atom bomb, especially on civilian targets. But in 1945, the public backed Truman. "To invade Japan would have cost an untold number of American lives—and Japanese lives," says Bob Baldridge.

Within a week, Japan accepted defeat, although Americans did not officially rejoice until September 2, V-J (Victory in Japan) Day. On that day, a Japanese government official boarded the U.S. battleship *Missouri* and signed over the administration of his country to General MacArthur. Halfway around the world, Wave Lee Lund hitchhiked into Washington, D.C. "It was body to body," she says. "And we were singing on the White House lawn. It was the greatest thing—champagne glasses in one hand, [champagne] glasses in the other."

Americans march into Paris in a Victory Parade, held to celebrate the liberation of France from Nazi occupation.

A HERO'S WELCOME

On the road to this victory, in 1944 and 1945, GIs fought some of the bloodiest battles of World War II. They also made many foreign friends. Unlike the Germans and the Japanese, the Allies invaded countries not to conquer but to liberate them. Even the Italians, whose government had sided with the Axis until 1943, welcomed Americans.

During German or Japanese occupation, many citizens in countries like France and the Philippines had joined underground fighting forces, known as the Resistance. Resistance fighters harassed the enemy, and when the Allies landed, they aided GIs. The Resistance knew the terrain and warned of Axis traps, such as mine fields.

As GIs marched though Europe, Resistance fighters and ordinary civilians thanked them with all their hearts. In village after village, locals greeted the troops by cheering and waving handkerchiefs. Journalist Ernie Pyle rode into Paris with the army in August 1944, and he called the outpouring of gratitude "the loveliest, brightest story of our time":

> Everybody kissed us—little children, old women, grown-up men, beautiful girls. They jumped and squealed and pushed in a literal frenzy. They pinned bright little flags and badges all over you. Amateur cameramen took pictures. They tossed flowers and friendly tomatoes into your jeep. One little girl even threw a bottle of cider into ours.

Although the fighting didn't get easier toward the war's end, the living did. After months of washing their own greasy coveralls, Bill Folley and other members of his bombing group hired some Italians to do their laundry. The lack of prejudice in much of Europe surprised and touched African Americans. A French Resistance officer, Henri, saw George Coar's all-black tank destroyer unit "sleeping out in an apple orchard in big tents and laying in the snow. So he helped us to find hay to put in the tents from barns of the farming people around there." After sunset Coar and four buddies gathered up rations and went to Henri's farmhouse. "His wife would cook up nice, warm meals for us," Coar recalls. "We would sleep there around the fireplace or stove and get up early and go

Allied POWs cheer as navy troops reach them at a Japanese prison camp on August 29, 1945.

back." In the United States in the 1940s, most white families would not have invited a black soldier into their homes.

Despite the gifts pressed into their hands, Americans found Europe in desperate poverty. Five years of war had not only leveled cities but had also destroyed national economies. Food, clothing, and fuel were scarce. All over the world, natives reused American garbage, wearing GI mattress covers as capes or smoking tobacco collected from cigarette butts. Kids tagged along behind the friendly strangers who passed out chocolate bars and chewing gum. In Italy villagers brought pots and pans to American camps to collect dinner leftovers. Troops also worked out deals—they donated their rations to local housewives and then sat down with the family for a home-cooked meal. Sometimes GIs stole coal and cans of meat from military stores to give away to civilians.

Although the army and the navy discouraged individual Robin Hoods, as organizations they tried to help liberated villages. Engineers repaired power and water lines. Doctors treated sick children. The Army Service Forces gave jobs to foreign civilians. Despite some problems with greedy or drunken GIs, liberation created personal and long-lasting bonds between Americans and the people they came to rescue.

American forces also freed Allied POWs, airlifting food and clothing as a message of hope until the ground troops arrived. "When it was over, the planes came in and started dropping chow," recalls Lou Curtis. At his prison camp in Japan, sorrow interrupted joy when a 50-gallon drum on a parachute hit and killed four Americans playing cards. "After going through all that," Curtis says, shaking his head, "to get killed by a crate of shoes."

As GIs crashed through prison fences in their tanks, they were shocked by the sight of inmates more dead than alive—civilians as well as soldiers. Allied outrage grew as troops entered European concentration camps where Nazis had gassed or worked to death six million Jewish adults and children. Among the corpses buried in ditches or stacked like firewood wandered survivors with numbers tattooed on their wrists.

Bob Baldridge's mortar battalion liberated a slave labor camp outside the city of Nordhausen. There, the Germans had built underground V-2 rocket factories, which they staffed with about 30,000 displaced persons— Hungarians, Poles, and Russians forced to leave their homes. When Bob Baldridge walked into the Nordhausen camp, the remaining prisoners were "just hanging around" with no idea what to do:

> They were emaciated living skeletons with vacant stares.... They were just out of it, mentally and physically. And they showed no emotion or no friendliness or anything about being liberated because they just weren't in shape to realize what was happening. . . .

Army medics provided health care, but many prisoners died not long after liberation. Under orders of General Dwight Eisenhower, U.S. troops rounded up Germans in nearby towns—everyone from the mayor to 10-year-old children—and marched them through concentration camps to view the horrors. "They knew damn well what was going on in that camp," says Bob Baldridge, "although they closed their eyes to it, closed their ears to it, and tried to forget about it."

"IT'S BEEN A LONG, LONG TIME"

In the fall of 1945, with the war won and their job done, most GIs longed to trade their uniforms for civilian clothes. "While the war was still on, I was very excited to be a part of it," says Bob Baldridge. "However, the minute the war in Europe was over, I could hardly wait to get home."

In three years, the military had dispersed Americans all over the globe. They couldn't all return to the United States at once. Even after the shooting ended, some troops had to perform "occupation" duty—to keep the peace while the Allies tried war criminals and helped new democratic governments take hold in Germany and Japan.

While commanders ordered GIs not to "fraternize," to make friends with their former enemies, troops had no desire to punish them either. In fact, soldiers often pitied the German and Japanese civilians who had suffered. Sergeant Joe McCarthy described in *Yank* the uncomfortable feeling of walking into Hiroshima in an American uniform, past the "hollow, blackened shell" of the hospital, past people "pointing at ashes that evidently used to be the homes of relatives or friends."

A marine finds a Japanese mother and her children hidden in a cave. Fierce fighting had forced the family to flee their home on Saipan.

In Germany, as a favor to one of his teachers from college back in the United States, Bob Baldridge set out in his jeep to look up a German professor. Baldridge found him living in an apartment in a bombed-out block in Munich: "He said, 'I lost all my books. I lost almost all of my clothes. I lost my dog. Oh, and I lost my wife.' Poor guy was shell-shocked." Baldridge gave him cans of food and cartons of cigarettes:

> There weren't any stores open and no way to get anything except by barter. Civilians like him in the city could buy food that was being brought in on little wheelbarrows and trucks and bicycles from the fields. . . . The way you got that from the farmers, the currency was cigarettes. So my two cartons of cigarettes probably saved him for the next month.

To determine which soldiers to discharge first, the military used a point system. An individual earned points for parenthood (12 for each child), overseas service, combat, and length of time in uniform (1 per month). At first GIs needed 85 points for a ticket home. With only 83 points on V-E Day, Bill Folley had to transfer to a B-17 unit in Italy to collect a few more. Even then, he and more than 100 other troops waited

A discharged GI is reunited with his wife and daughter.

for a couple of weeks in Naples before boarding a ship because no one could find their records. "Eventually they found out that there was a Wac who was typing the records, and her chair was not quite high enough to be comfortable for typing, so she sat on 110 of our records."

All along the journey, impatient Americans put up with crowded transportation and long lines. Although airplanes flew POWs and some troops to ports in Europe and Asia, everyone had to cross the oceans again by ship. Bill Folley traveled home from Italy on an ocean liner captured from the Germans. It was so packed that some GIs slept outside on the deck. Anticipation—hopes for a happy homecoming—ran high. Although troops also worried about the future, excitement overwhelmed other emotions. Folley remembers steaming into New York:

> As we started to see land, we saw all these big signs, Cokes and so forth, and it was right near Coney Island. . . . The old Statue of Liberty looked great; it was all brightened up. And the fireboats were sailing around, blowing water up and down.

No families met GIs at the dock, however. Before official discharge, troops reported to "separation centers," camps and forts once used for training. There, after a good steak dinner, soldiers underwent medical tests, and instructors informed troops about the GI Bill. Passed by Congress in June 1944, the bill guaranteed male and female service personnel free college tuition, low-interest loans to buy a home or business, and a readjustment allowance—dubbed the "52-20" club because veterans could collect $20 a week for a year.

And then, finally, GIs went home. In the midst of millions of joyful family reunions, many veterans struggled to make the transition back to civilian life. Wave Martha Abramson recalls:

> I got out of the service . . . and people [had] moved during the war. My mom and dad left our hometown, and they moved down to Florida. . . . All of a sudden, I don't know anybody. It was miserable. I didn't know what I wanted to do. . . . Can you imagine these fellows that get out and are blind, or lost a leg?

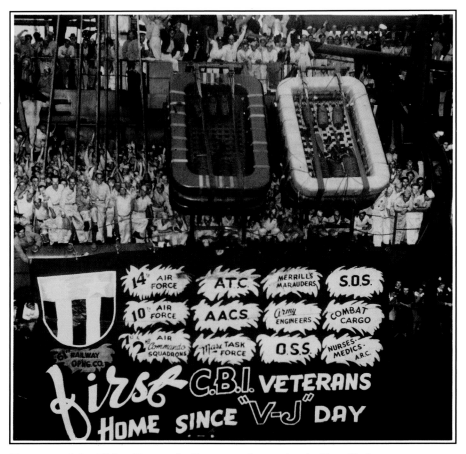

Veterans of the China-Burma-India campaign arrive in New York on September 27, 1945.

Everyone had lost something—if not a limb, perhaps a friend, a brother, a sense of innocence. Trying to forget the horrors of combat, some veterans drank or partied too hard. With food and rest, Lou Curtis regained his health. But as an ex-POW, "I had this big part of my life taken out of it," he says. "It took a while to get readjusted. And we were a little loose with our money."

Women on the home front had grown more independent between 1941 and 1945, a change that many male veterans didn't appreciate. In addition to managing households while their husbands served in uniform, many wives had also taken jobs in defense plants or other "male" workplaces. As life returned to "normal," female workers often resented losing the opportunities that had opened during the war. Some veterans felt the same way. Wacs and Waves often missed the camaraderie, pay, and prestige of the service.

For black soldiers, too, especially those exposed to the racial tolerance of Europe, continuing prejudice in the United States insulted their dignity. Hadn't black Americans fought and died for their country? During separation at Fort MacPherson, Georgia, officers sat down with a group of soldiers to discuss readjustment. George Coar remembers that when someone complained about a lack of choices for black veterans, a white Southerner made a racist remark. One black soldier murmured in response, "And the war begins now." African Americans had another battle ahead—the civil rights movement of the 1950s and 1960s.

Despite social change and racial conflict in the postwar years, the shared experience of World War II shaped the outlook of a whole generation of Americans. In best-selling novels, writers like Norman Mailer (*The Naked and the Dead*), Kurt Vonnegut (*Slaughterhouse Five*), and Joseph Heller (*Catch-22*) reflected on the cruelty and waste of combat. Yet most Americans believed that the Allies had fought for a just cause and that their sacrifices had brightened the future. Veterans who entered politics continued to promote the United States as the world's chief defender of democracy. Every president elected between 1952 and 1988— from Dwight Eisenhower, an army general in Europe, to George Bush, a naval pilot in the Pacific—served in the military during World War II.

As quickly and willingly as they had learned how to soldier, American men and women embraced peace and the prosperity that followed in the 1950s. Some veterans returned to their old jobs. More took advantage of the GI Bill to enroll in school, start a business, or buy a house in the suburbs. "It's impossible to forget [the war] entirely," says Charles Ives, "but you got to still go on living." With little fuss and few parades, GIs put away their uniforms and became civilians again. "A pat on the back," says BettyLou Folley. "The war was over."

SELECTED BIBLIOGRAPHY

Boardman, Barrington. *Flappers, Bootleggers, "Typhoid Mary," and the Bomb: An Anecdotal History of the United States from 1923-1945.* New York: Harper & Row, 1988.

Bourke-White, Margaret. *Portrait of Myself.* Boston: G. K. Hall & Co., 1963/1985.

Gordon, Lois and Alan. *American Chronicle: Seven Decades in American Life.* New York: Crown Publishers, Inc., 1987.

Gurney, Gene and Clare. *Women on the March.* New York: Abelard-Schuman, 1975.

Harris, Mark Jonathan, et al. *The Homefront: America During World War II.* New York: G. P. Putnam's Sons, 1984.

Hartmann, Susan M. *American Women in the 1940s: The Home Front and Beyond.* Boston: Twayne Publishers, 1982.

Keegan, John. *The Second World War.* New York: Viking, 1990.

Kennett, Lee. *G.I.: The American Soldier in World War II.* New York: Charles Scribner's Sons, 1987.

Kluger, Steve. *Yank: The Army Weekly.* New York: St. Martin's Press, 1991.

Litoff, Judy Barrett et al. *Miss You: The World War II Letters of Barbara Wooddall Taylor and Charles E. Taylor.* Athens, Georgia: The University of Georgia Press, 1990.

Mauldin, Bill. *Up Front.* New York: Henry Holt and Company, 1945.

McGuire, Phillip. *Taps for a Jim Crow Army*. Santa Barbara, California: ABC-Clio, Inc., 1983.

Pyle, Ernie. *Brave Men*. New York: Henry Holt and Company, 1944.

Ravitch, Diane, ed. *The American Reader: Words That Moved a Nation*. New York: HarperCollins, 1990.

Steinberg, Rafael. *Island Fighting*. Chicago: Time-Life Books, 1978.

Sulzberger, C. L. *World War II*. Boston: Houghton Mifflin Company, 1966.

Swineford, Edwin J. *Wits of War: Unofficial GI Humor-History of World War II*. Fresno, California: Kilroy Was There Press, 1989.

Terkel, Studs. *"The Good War": An Oral History of World War Two*. New York: Ballantine Books, 1984.

Verges, Marianne. *On Silver Wings: The Women Airforce Service Pilots of World War II 1941-1944*. New York: Ballantine Books, 1991.

Also by Sylvia Whitman

V Is for Victory:
The American Home Front during World War II
Lerner Publications Company, 1993

INDEX

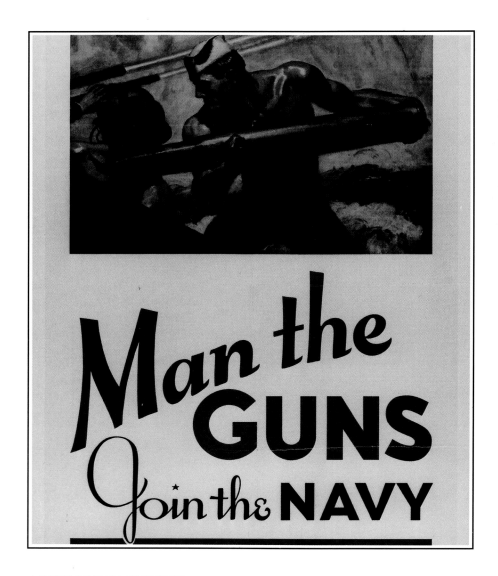

ACKNOWLEDGMENTS

Photographs and illustrations reproduced with permission of the National Archives except, pp. 6, 19, 72: Virginia State Library and Archives; p. 7: Library of Congress; pp. 9, 10 (left), 12: United Press International; pp. 15, 78: Kansas State Historical Society; p. 16: U.S. Naval Historical Center; p. 18: Women Airforce Service Pilots; p. 20: Smithsonian Institution; p. 27: Hollywood Book and Poster; p. 64 (bottom): Lou Curtis. Front cover: National Archives. Back cover: Smithsonian Institution.